Made for you
WINTER

**SEASONAL RECIPES FOR GIFTS
AND CELEBRATIONS**

About Sophie

Born and raised in Sydney, now living with her family on their farm just outside Orange in country New South Wales, Sophie Hansen trained in journalism and has over 20 years' experience as a features writer. She has contributed to *Australian Country Style* and *Outback* magazines; she was an editor for Slow Food International's English website, lived in Italy for 3 years and is fluent in Italian. In 2013 she set up her blog, *Local is Lovely*, and her podcast, *My Open Kitchen*, is going into its third season. Sophie has been awarded Australian Rural Woman of the Year in recognition of her commitment to rural communities. She believes in simple, tasty and seasonal food, made with love and shared generously.

Instagram: @locallovely @myopenkitchen

Made for you
you
WINTER

SEASONAL RECIPES FOR GIFTS
AND CELEBRATIONS

Make ~ Wrap ~ Deliver

Sophie Hansen

murdoch books
Sydney | London

CONTENTS

Food for thought

A lovely lady recently told me about love bombing. She and her friend have an agreement that when things get difficult, they make up a casserole or cake or whatever, drop it off at the other's front door and send a quick text saying 'incoming love bomb' before driving away. There's no pressure to open the door and be hospitable when that might be the very last thing you feel capable of doing – just the understanding that someone is thinking of you, there for you and making good food for you.

This story really is the essence of this little book. It's about how cooking for your friends and family is the very best thing you can do for them, in good times and bad. It's about bringing people together at a table for a warming kitchen supper or taking them a lasagne layered with winter greens or organising a weekend away in the country with friends and lots of delicious, easy food – these are the gestures and moments that matter most.

And because winter is a time for rich braises, for sweet yeasted doughs, for bright citrus jellies and curds, and bolstering breakfasts before big days of sport or work in the freezing cold, that's just what this book brings you. There are recipes to make for friends laid low with colds and flu, filling and delicious soups, curries, dahl, baked beans, baked porridge and more. This is grounding, warming, loved-up food that you can make for your friends and your own family.

All of the recipes are designed to be doubled, so you can (and will, I hope) be making up good things to share with friends in need and also fill your own fridge, pantry and biscuit jars. They are easy to make, delicious to eat and perfect for sharing.

Packing up your care parcels

I think that if you are going to take the time to make a beautiful casserole, cake or jar of biscuits for someone, a few more minutes styling that gift up so it looks as good as it will undoubtedly taste are minutes well spent! Big tea towels or fabric offcuts are perfect for wrapping up cakes, boxes, bottles and even casserole dishes. And they look extra good when tied up with some kitchen string or ribbon with a posy of herbs or winter blooms tucked into the fabric folds.

One way to be sure you always have something cute to wrap or style up your edible gifts is to keep a drawer, shelf or basket aside in your kitchen or pantry with a little stash of fabrics and ribbons and cards. And please, when you are making a meal for a friend in need, don't give it away in your best, most expensive container – the last thing you'll want to do is pester them to get it back. Stock up on retro casserole dishes from your local opportunity shop, buy foil containers from the shops or just gift a container that you don't mind never seeing again.

Practical tips for giving food

Winter is a good time to be making and dropping off edible care packages – much less need for ice bricks and cool bags when the temperature outside is as cold as the fridge. Nevertheless, it's better to be safe than sorry. Here are a few rules of thumb to keep in mind when preparing, storing and transporting food: wash your hands before cooking and be aware of safe temperatures and storage times. Once cooked, cool food on the bench until steam stops rising, then place it in the fridge. Don't let food cool completely on the bench. And don't put hot food straight into

There are lots of fun, easy ways to make your edible gifts look gorgeous.

the freezer – cool it in the fridge first. Cooked food can generally be safely stored in the fridge for 3 to 4 days only.

To freeze casseroles, divide them into servings of a size that suits your family or the family they are heading to, then place in freezer-safe containers or bags, label with the name of the dish and date, and freeze for 2 to 3 months. Avoid freezer burn by using good thick, resealable bags or quality containers and leave a couple of centimetres at the top of the bag or container to allow the food to expand when frozen. The best and safest place to thaw frozen food is in the fridge.

Watercolour gift tags

Winter is the perfect time to get crafting, and even if you are no artist (I'm definitely not!) there are lots of fun, easy things you can do to make your edible gifts look as gorgeous as they taste. My favourite is to create simple line drawings on the labels of my jams or preserves or cake tags and colour them in with watercolour paints. It's such a simple task but they look really lovely and are super satisfying to create. Pinterest is a great place to find some inspiration for food labels and wrapping. Get creative and have fun!

Beeswax food wraps

These wraps have become popular in recent years as a smart, eco-friendly alternative to plastic wrap. And while you can find them in shops, beeswax wraps are usually fairly expensive. But here's the good news: they're super cheap and easy to make. So grab some fabric (an old shirt or pillowcase) and make up a bunch of wraps to give away as presents

and/or wrap gifts, sandwiches for school lunches, cover bowls of leftovers and so on.

You'll need 200 g (7 oz) solid beeswax (find it online or in speciality stores), 1 tablespoon olive oil, pinking shears, an old paintbrush, baking paper, a few baking trays and 6–8 fabric rectangles (they'll need to fit on your baking trays, so use that as a size guide).

Preheat the oven to 150°C (300°F). Line your baking trays with baking paper and place a piece of fabric on each. Melt the beeswax in a glass bowl over a pan of simmering water, stir in the oil, then brush it over the fabric. Pop in the oven for a few minutes, then brush again so the wax evenly and lightly covers the fabric. Hang on a clothesline to dry and they're ready to use. Wash beeswax wraps in lukewarm water, never in the dishwasher! If you find them a bit stiff, just work with your hands for a minute until the warmth makes them pliable.

Dahl for your darlings

Oven-roasted chicken curry ~ Simple vegetable dahl
Sweet potato, lime and tamarind curry

Oh, dahl; equal parts delicious, healthy, cheap and easy to make, dahl ticks every box.
And even though this little selection of recipes only features one dahl proper, all three
recipes would be perfect to make and give to someone needing warming nourishment.
Together they form a fantastic feast but each one also stands alone as a meal,
perhaps with some steamed white or brown rice.

OVEN-ROASTED CHICKEN CURRY

This grounding, warming curry is a meal in itself, with the split peas adding sustenance to keep you feeling full. I make it fairly mild so that everyone can enjoy it, then add a good sprinkle of fresh or dried chilli to mine at the table, along with a dollop of yoghurt. I think cooking this in the oven rather than on the stovetop produces a far richer, thicker curry, but you could take the stovetop option. Just keep the temperature low and the lid slightly off. The spice paste is worth having on hand in the fridge – simply rub it over chicken or lamb before barbecuing, or use it as a marinade.

2 Tbsp coconut oil
2 brown onions, diced
700 g (1 lb 9 oz) skinless chicken
    thigh fillets, cut into 3 cm
    (1 1/4 inch) pieces
1/2 cup (130 g) Greek-style yoghurt,
    plus extra to serve
2 Tbsp tomato paste (concentrated
    purée)
680 g (1 lb 8 oz) jar tomato passata
3 cups (750 ml) chicken stock
1 cup (205 g) chana dahl (split
    yellow lentils), soaked in cold
    water for at least 1 hour
2 handfuls English spinach
Toasted slivered almonds, to serve
Steamed rice, to serve

Spice paste
5 green cardamom pods
2 cloves
1 cinnamon stick
4 black peppercorns
4 garlic cloves, peeled
1 thumb-sized piece ginger,
    roughly chopped
1 thumb-sized piece turmeric,
    roughly chopped, or 1 tsp
    ground turmeric
1 Tbsp ground cumin
1 tsp ground coriander
A good pinch of chilli flakes,
    or to taste
2 Tbsp coconut oil

For the spice paste, combine the cardamom pods, cloves, cinnamon stick and peppercorns in a dry frying pan and toast for a few minutes or until fragrant. Transfer to a food processor, spice grinder or mortar and pestle and bash/blitz until well ground. Add the garlic, ginger, turmeric, cumin, coriander, chilli and coconut oil and bash/blitz again until combined.

Preheat the oven to 130°C (250°F). Heat the coconut oil in a large ovenproof saucepan or flameproof casserole dish over medium heat. Cook the onion for 7–10 minutes or until soft and translucent. Add the spice paste and cook, stirring constantly, for a few minutes. Bump up the heat to high, add the chicken and cook for 3–4 minutes to seal.

Add 1 tablespoon of the yoghurt, stirring well so all the flavours mix together and the yoghurt dries somewhat, then repeat with another tablespoon of yoghurt and another until it's all incorporated. Stir in the tomato paste and cook for another minute.

Add the passata and stir until the chicken is well coated in the spiced yoghurt mixture. Cook for 5 minutes, then pour in the stock and chana dahl and stir well. Transfer to the oven and cook for 3 hours, stirring every now and then so it doesn't stick to the bottom of the pan.

Stir in the spinach and serve the curry with slivered almonds, yoghurt and steamed rice.

SERVES 6

SIMPLE VEGETABLE DAHL

There are countless variations of dahl; this is mine – easy, mellow and tasty. Serve it with steamed brown rice and/or naan, a dollop of yoghurt or just on its own. I add a good sprinkle of chilli and a squeeze of lime or lemon juice.

1 Tbsp coconut oil, ghee or olive oil
1 brown onion, diced
1 cup (205 g) red lentils
1 Tbsp ground cumin
1 Tbsp ground turmeric
1 Tbsp garam masala
3 garlic cloves, finely chopped
4 cm (1 1/2 inch) piece ginger, peeled
   and finely chopped
1 bunch coriander (cilantro)
1 carrot, finely diced
2 celery stalks, finely chopped
4 cups (1 litre) water or stock

Heat the oil in a large saucepan over medium–high heat. Cook the onion, stirring, for a few minutes, then add the lentils, spices, garlic and ginger. Finely chop the coriander stalks and add these to the pan, along with most of the leaves (save some to garnish). Cook, stirring often, for about 10 minutes.

Add the carrot and celery and cook for a few minutes more. Pour in the water or stock, then reduce the heat and cook for 45 minutes or until the vegetables have softened completely and the lentils are tender. Add more water or stock if you feel like the dahl needs to loosen up a bit. Serve garnished with the reserved coriander leaves.

SERVES 6–8

SWEET POTATO, LIME AND TAMARIND CURRY

This curry is influenced by one of Anna Jones's recipes in her wonderful book, *A Modern Way to Cook*. I'm an enormous fan of this British food writer and her recipes are on high rotation in our house. Fresh but warming at the same time, it's a gorgeous dish. One of the army of recipe testers that I enlisted to help with this book suggested adding a cup of red lentils with the sweet potato. She also stirred through a few handfuls of greens right at the end, which is a great idea – thanks, Rachel!

1 Tbsp coconut oil or vegetable oil
1 brown onion, diced
1 bunch coriander (cilantro)
2 garlic cloves, finely chopped
3 cm (1 1/4 inch) piece ginger, peeled and
   finely chopped
600 g (1 lb 5 oz) sweet potato, peeled
   and cut into 3 cm (1 1/4 inch) cubes
1 tsp mustard seeds
2 x 400 g (14 oz) tins chopped tomatoes
2 x 400 g (14 oz) tins coconut milk
2 Tbsp tamarind paste
Juice of 1 lime
1 tsp soft brown sugar
Steamed brown rice, to serve

Heat the oil in a large flameproof casserole dish or saucepan over medium–high heat. Cook the onion, stirring often, for 5 minutes. Snip the leaves from the coriander and thinly slice the stalks. Add the garlic, ginger and coriander stalks to the pan and cook for another couple of minutes. Now add the sweet potato and mustard seeds and cook, stirring often, for a few more minutes.

Stir in the tomatoes, coconut milk, tamarind paste, lime juice and brown sugar. Bring to a simmer, then cook for 30 minutes or until the sweet potato is tender. Check and adjust the flavour.

Serve with the coriander leaves and steamed brown rice. Store in the fridge for up to a week, or freeze.

SERVES 4–6

Weekend in the country

Friday night: Anna's minestrone ~ Alice's garlic bread

Saturday breakfast: Baked butterbeans with fried eggs and/or Baked apple porridge

Saturday lunch: Chops and sausages with Pearl barley, beetroot and yoghurt salad

Saturday dinner: Braised fennel and tomato ~ Light and crunchy winter salad ~ Rich lasagne with winter greens
Ginger and pear pudding with Salted caramel sauce (page 75) and ice cream

Sunday breakfast: Fluffy pancakes with Poached quinces (page 75) and Sweet dukkah (page 74)

Winter weekends away with friends or at home with a houseful of visitors are my favourite. And here's why: most of our catch-ups these days seem to be on borrowed time – a quick coffee with a friend before work, half an hour for lunch to swap news and stories in rapid fire or, if we're lucky, a long lunch or dinner over the weekend. So the chance to spend a whole weekend with your favourite people is extra special. As are the good chats to be had while washing up, out for a Saturday morning walk, over a card game or during a car trip. So please, once a year if you can, beg, borrow, steal or rent a house with a group of buddies, get them all to commit to a weekend in winter and lock it in. A week out, delegate a meal per person. People are always happy to contribute if there's a team leader who's happy to delegate and make sure that not everyone brings lasagne.

My second suggestion for a great weekend away is to get some games happening. My friends think I'm a total games tragic – I walk into a room of people relaxing by the fire and instantly feel the need to organise them into some kind of activity. Charades, gin rummy, Scrabble, celebrity head; it doesn't matter what it is, as long as there's a competition underway. And while they tease me for not letting them be, it's pretty clear once the charades start, and the laughter and noise wakes up the kids, that everyone secretly loves it.

And a third tip for good weekends away: organise an outdoor activity for Saturday afternoon – a bonfire, bushwalk, game of cricket, hide and seek, whatever. Better yet, take your lunch out for a picnic. There's nothing better than coming in, all red-faced, happily exerted and hungry from the cool fresh air, to stoke the fire, pour the red wine and heat up your lasagne.

The menu

Most of the dishes on my menu can be made before the weekend and brought along to be worked into a meal. For example, with the lasagne, someone can make the ragu during the week and bring it along with lasagne sheets and the white sauce ingredients so it's more of an assembly job on the day. The minestrone, garlic bread, pudding and quinces can all be made before the weekend and then just heated, baked and gussied up a bit before serving.

This delicious, filling soup will keep everyone going.

ANNA'S MINESTRONE

This is the perfect winter soup – hearty, tasty, full of veggies and super healthy. The recipe comes via my friend Anna, who is an excellent cook and can always be counted on to bring the goods to any gathering.

1 bunch basil
2 Tbsp olive oil
4 rashers smoky bacon, cut into strips
2 red onions, diced
1 swede, peeled and diced
1 parsnip, peeled and diced
2 carrots, peeled and diced
2 celery stalks, diced
3 garlic cloves, finely chopped
2 x 400 g (14 oz) tins chopped tomatoes
3 cups (750 ml) chicken or vegetable stock
1 glass red wine
1 handful pearl barley
½ cup (100 g) risoni pasta
400 g (14 oz) tin cannellini beans, drained
1 bunch English spinach, stalks removed, shredded
Shaved parmesan cheese, to serve
Extra virgin olive oil, for drizzling

Pick the basil leaves from the stalks and set aside. Finely chop the stalks.

Heat the oil in a large saucepan over medium–high heat. Add the bacon, onion, swede, parsnip, carrot, celery, garlic and basil stalks. Reduce the heat to low and sweat the bacon and vegetables, stirring occasionally, for 15 minutes or until softened.

Add the tomatoes, stock, wine and barley to the pan and simmer for 20 minutes. Add the risoni and cannellini beans, stir well and cook for 10 minutes or until the barley and risoni are tender. Stir in the spinach and cook for a minute or so until just wilted. Season to taste.

Serve the minestrone topped with the finely chopped basil leaves, parmesan and a good drizzle of olive oil.

SERVES 8

ALICE'S GARLIC BREAD

My Alice just adores garlic bread (actually, doesn't everyone?), but especially this one. It can be prepared and left in the fridge, wrapped with foil and ready to be baked, for up to 4 days.

3 garlic cloves, peeled
100 g (3½ oz) butter, softened
1 handful flat-leaf parsley, finely chopped
¼ cup (25 g) finely grated parmesan cheese
1 baguette or loaf of nice bread

Combine the garlic, butter, parsley and parmesan with some salt and pepper in a food processor and whizz to combine, or place in a mortar and bash around with the pestle until combined.

Cut the bread into 3 cm (1¼ inch) slices, without cutting all the way through. Spread a little garlic butter on each slice, then spread any extra over the top of the baguette.

Tightly wrap the baguette in foil and keep in the fridge until ready to bake. When that time comes, preheat the oven to 200°C (400°F). Cook the wrapped baguette for 30 minutes, then open up the foil so the top of the baguette is exposed and cook it for another 15 minutes or until golden. Serve warm.

SERVES 4–6

BAKED BUTTERBEANS
WITH FRIED EGGS

I love a breakfast picnic, especially a mid-winter one when everyone rugs up and huddles around a fire to watch the sun rise. Of course, this would also be delicious served in a cosy, warm kitchen.

2–3 Tbsp olive oil, plus extra for drizzling
200 g (7 oz) bacon, cut into small pieces
1 brown onion, diced
1 garlic clove, finely chopped
1 Tbsp soft brown sugar
1 cinnamon stick
1/4 tsp ground cumin
1/4 tsp mixed spice
2 x 400 g (14 oz) tins chopped tomatoes
2 Tbsp Worcestershire sauce
2 cups (380 g) dried butterbeans, soaked overnight
   in cold water, then cooked until completely
   tender, or 400 g (14 oz) tin butterbeans, rinsed
   and drained
1 fried egg per person
Chopped flat-leaf parsley, to serve
Chilli flakes, to serve (optional)

Preheat the oven to 160°C (320°F).

Pour 2 tablespoons of the olive oil into a heavy-based ovenproof saucepan or flameproof casserole dish. Add the bacon and cook over medium–high heat until nice and crispy. Remove with a slotted spoon and set aside.

Reduce the heat to medium–low, add a little more olive oil and cook the onion and garlic until soft and translucent, about 5 minutes. Add the sugar, spices and a good seasoning of sea salt and black pepper. Cook for a few minutes more.

Add the tomatoes, cooked bacon, 1/2 cup (125 ml) water (or more if you think it's looking at all dry) and the Worcestershire sauce. Bring to the boil, then stir in the butterbeans. Cover with a lid or tight-fitting layer of foil and place in the oven for 45 minutes to 1 hour or until warmed through and bubbling.

Serve topped with the fried eggs, a drizzle of olive oil, lots of chopped parsley and a few chilli flakes.

SERVES 6–8

BAKED APPLE PORRIDGE

Baked porridge is a bit of a breakfast game changer. No stirring, no burnt pots, just one big tray of goodness. Plus it feels like having dessert for breakfast. You can use any fruit you like here. I usually use tart granny smith apples, but while testing for this book I also made this with fresh strawberries and poached quinces. Both were big hits. It's also lovely served sprinkled with Sweet dukkah (page 74).

Put this together before you go to bed and leave it in the fridge, or just throw it together before breakfast. If you're preparing it in the morning, you may need to cook it for an extra 5 to 10 minutes.

4 cooking apples, peeled and thinly sliced or grated
1 ½ cups (150 g) rolled oats (not instant)
1 tsp ground cinnamon
1 tsp baking powder
A pinch of salt
¼ cup (45 g) soft brown sugar
⅓ cup (40 g) toasted walnuts, hazelnuts or
    almonds, roughly chopped
2 eggs
4 cups (1 litre) full-cream milk
1 tsp vanilla bean paste
Plain yoghurt and honey, to serve

Preheat the oven to 180°C (350°F). Lightly grease a 6 cup (1.5 litre) ovenproof dish. Spread the apple over the base of the dish.

Combine the oats with the cinnamon, baking powder, salt, sugar and nuts, then sprinkle the mixture over the apple.

Whisk the eggs, milk and vanilla bean paste together and pour over the oat mixture. (At this point, you can cover the dish and place it in the fridge overnight.)

Bake for 1 hour or until the top is turning golden and the porridge is still slightly wobbly in the middle. Serve with yoghurt and a drizzle of honey.

SERVES 6-8

BRAISED FENNEL
AND TOMATO

A gorgeous, easy wintery dish, this recipe can
be taken in all sorts of directions. Serve it as a
side dish with the lasagne and winter salad as
I've suggested, or as a main meal on soft polenta
with a green salad. Try it tossed through pasta or
spooned over toasted sourdough and topped
with a crumble of feta cheese.

1/4 cup (60 ml) olive oil
6 fennel bulbs, trimmed and cut into quarters
2 brown onions, diced
3 garlic cloves, finely chopped
6 anchovy fillets, roughly chopped
1/4 cup (45 g) green olives, pitted and
  roughly chopped
1 cup (250 ml) white wine
2 x 400 g (14 oz) tins whole peeled tomatoes,
  or 800 g (1 lb 12 oz) ripe, fresh tomatoes,
  cut into quarters
1/4 cup (45 g) capers, rinsed
1 handful flat-leaf parsley leaves

Heat half the oil in a large heavy-based saucepan
over medium–high heat. Add the fennel quarters,
in batches if necessary, and cook until browned
on all sides. Remove from the pan and set aside.

Reduce the heat a little and add the remaining oil.
Cook the onion for 10 minutes or until soft and
translucent. Add the garlic, anchovies and olives
and cook, stirring often, for a few more minutes.
Pour in the wine and cook, stirring often, until
reduced by half.

Return the fennel quarters to the pan, add the
tomatoes and capers and simmer for 40 minutes.
Serve sprinkled with the parsley.

SERVES 8 (AS A SIDE DISH)

PEARL BARLEY, BEETROOT
AND YOGHURT SALAD

A really yummy, healthy salad, this is great for
a picnic or buffet lunch as it sits around happily
for ages and tastes great at room temperature.

3 beetroot, cut into quarters
1/2 cup (125 ml) olive oil
1 1/2 cups (300 g) pearl barley
6 cups (1.5 litres) boiling water
2 Tbsp apple cider vinegar
Grated zest and juice of 1 lemon
1/4 cup (40 g) sunflower seeds
1/4 cup (40 g) pine nuts
1 bunch dill, finely chopped
1 cup (260 g) Greek-style yoghurt

Preheat the oven to 200°C (400°F). Put the beetroot
quarters on a baking tray, drizzle with a little of the
olive oil and sprinkle with salt and pepper. Roast for
40 minutes or until tender.

Meanwhile, combine the barley and 2 tablespoons
of the olive oil in a large saucepan over medium–high
heat. Toast, stirring often, for 10 minutes. Pour in the
boiling water and boil until tender, about 15 minutes.

Mix together the remaining olive oil, vinegar, lemon
zest and lemon juice and season to taste.

Put the sunflower seeds and pine nuts in a dry frying
pan and toast over medium heat, tossing occasionally,
for 2 minutes or until golden.

As soon as you drain the barley, tip it into a large
bowl and mix in the dressing. Leave to cool for a few
minutes, then mix in the sunflower seeds, pine nuts
and dill. Top with the roasted beetroot (even better
if it's still warm) and yoghurt, and season to taste.

SERVES 6

LIGHT AND CRUNCHY WINTER SALAD

The idea here is to offer a fresh, crunchy alternative to the richer mains on offer, so chop up a few baby
cos lettuce heads and toss with some sliced radishes, cucumbers and snow peas. Crumble some feta
cheese over the top and dress with a drizzle of olive oil and a splash or two of white wine vinegar.
Sprinkle with some crushed up Roasted fennel and chilli nuts (page 51).

RICH LASAGNE WITH WINTER GREENS

This lasagne is a bit of a labour of love, but well worth it. And for bonus points, it contains a good serve of greens. This recipe makes either one very large lasagne – I use an enamel lasagne tray that measures 25 x 38 x 7 cm (10 x 15 x 2¾ inches) – or two smaller ones. Please consider doubling the recipe and making two large or four small lasagnes.

THERE ARE FOUR STEPS TO THIS RECIPE

1. Make a double batch of the Spicy, smoky beef ragu from page 74. This can (and should) be done a day or at least a few hours before you want to assemble and bake the lasagne. Allow for about 3 hours in the oven.

2. Wilt the greens.

3. Make the white sauce (allow about 20 minutes).

4. Assemble and bake!

For the ragu
Pop over to page 74 and make a double quantity of that gorgeous, richly flavoured beef ragu.

For the greens
2 Tbsp olive oil
1 brown onion, diced
8 cups (about 450 g) mixed shredded greens
  (kale, English spinach and chard are all good)
A pinch of salt
A pinch of freshly ground black pepper

Heat the oil in a saucepan over medium–high heat. Cook the onion for about 5 minutes or until soft and translucent. Add the greens a few handfuls at a time, adding the salt and pepper as you go, and stirring so the greens wilt and allow room for more. Continue adding the greens and cook until they are just wilted. Set aside in the pan until assembly time.

For the white sauce
80 g (2¾ oz) butter
²/₃ cup (100 g) plain flour
4 cups (1 litre) milk, warmed
A pinch of freshly grated nutmeg
½ cup (50 g) grated parmesan cheese

Melt the butter in a saucepan over medium heat. Once it's bubbling, add the flour and cook for a few minutes, whisking all the time, until you have a thick paste. Add a ladleful of milk and whisk until smooth. Add a few more ladlefuls of milk, whisking until smooth. Continue until all of the milk has been incorporated. Cook, whisking often, for 5 minutes or until you have a smooth, thick sauce. Remove from the heat and whisk in the nutmeg and parmesan.

To assemble
350 g (12 oz) instant lasagne sheets
200 g (7 oz) mozzarella cheese, torn into
  small pieces
1 cup (100 g) grated parmesan cheese

Preheat the oven to 180°C (350°F).

Spread a third of the ragu over the base of a lasagne dish. Top with a layer of lasagne sheets, then a third of the white sauce and sprinkle with a third of the mozzarella and parmesan. Add half of the greens, then top with another third of the ragu. Top with some more lasagne sheets and another third of the white sauce and cheeses. Add the remaining greens and then the remaining ragu. Top with a final layer of lasagne sheets and the remaining white sauce.

Finish with the remaining cheeses and pop into the oven to cook for 40 minutes (or cover well and place in the fridge or freezer until needed).

NOTE
It's important that the ragu is only reheated once after it's cooked. If you're making this as a helpful present, assemble the lasagne but don't bake it – just include a note with the baking instructions.

SERVES 8–10

GINGER AND PEAR PUDDING

A classic and for good reason – this pudding can be made in advance, then warmed up when it's time for dessert. It's super delicious, comforting and easy to make. Serve it with Salted caramel sauce (page 75), gently warmed in a small saucepan over medium heat.

1 cup (160 g) pitted dates
1/2 cup (110 g) crystallised ginger
1 tsp bicarbonate of soda
1 1/2 cups (375 ml) boiling water
80 g (2 3/4 oz) butter, softened
3/4 cup (165 g) firmly packed soft
  brown sugar
2 eggs
1 tsp vanilla bean paste
1 1/2 cups (225 g) plain flour
1 tsp baking powder
1 tsp ground ginger
1/2 tsp ground cinnamon
3 pears, thinly sliced
Salted caramel sauce (page 75),
  to serve
Vanilla ice cream, to serve

Preheat the oven to 160°C (320°F). Grease and line a 25 cm (10 inch) round cake tin with baking paper.

Combine the dates, crystallised ginger and bicarbonate of soda in the bowl of your food processor and pour in the boiling water. Set aside for a few minutes.

Add the butter, sugar, eggs and vanilla to the food processor and whizz everything together for a few seconds. Now add the flour, baking powder and spices and whizz again so you have a smooth batter.

Pour the batter into the cake tin and top with the pear slices. Bake for 45 minutes or until the centre of the pudding feels springy and it is just starting to pull away from the side of the tin.

Serve the pudding warm, with the warm caramel sauce and a scoop or two of vanilla ice cream.

SERVES 8

End the day on a sweet note with this pudding – then a game of cards.

FLUFFY PANCAKES

Orange-based photographer and friend Pip Farquharson made these pancakes for breakfast at a workshop I co-hosted recently and they were a big fat hit. Fluffy, sweet and really the best way to start a lazy Sunday morning, don't you think?

3 eggs
2 Tbsp caster sugar
1 1/3 cups (200 g) self-raising flour
150 ml (5 fl oz) milk
50 g (1 3/4 oz) butter
Plain yoghurt, to serve
Sweet dukkah (page 74), to serve
Poached quinces (page 75), to serve

Whisk the eggs and sugar until light and fluffy, then fold in the flour, followed by the milk. Gently mix together until well combined.

Heat a knob of butter in a non-stick frying pan over medium heat. Drop a good dollop of the batter into the pan, cook for a few minutes until bubbles appear, then gently flip over to cook for another couple of minutes. Repeat with the remaining batter, cooking two or three at a time (depending on the size of your frying pan).

I've served these with a dollop of plain yoghurt, a good sprinkle of dukkah and some warm poached quinces on the side and they are DELICIOUS. Any of the following seasonal options would be lovely too:

~ Rhubarb compote (page 75) and toasted, crushed hazelnuts
~ Fresh berries
~ Sliced bananas, honey and toasted, crushed pecans
~ Fresh honeycomb and orange segments
~ Roasted vanilla strawberries with a little whipped cream or coconut cream.

SERVES 6

A tray in bed

Aromatic chicken pho ~ Ginger, lemon and turmeric super tonic ~ Spoonful of sunshine orange jelly

I remember one of the only good things about feeling sick when we were kids was that Mum let us eat dinner on a tray in bed. It seemed like such a treat to be allowed to eat in bed and have everything plated up and delivered as if we were some kind of very important person. There's something pretty lovely about having a tray of good things delivered bedside when you're feeling poorly, so here are a few options that you might like to make, deliver and administer next time one of your people is laid low with the flu or similar.

There's something lovely about having a tray delivered bedside when you're feeling poorly.

AROMATIC CHICKEN PHO

Since last year when we visited Vietnam as a family, this recipe has become our go-to chicken soup recipe, especially when people are feeling lacklustre. I don't for a second pretend that this is an authentic pho, rather our take on the concept of chicken cooked in an aromatic broth, served with noodles and herbs. It's clean and light, yet the broth is loaded with flavour.

There is a bit of time involved in this recipe, but ninety per cent of it is hands off and the result is one hundred per cent worth it.

3 brown onions, roughly chopped
4 garlic cloves, halved
4 cm (1 1/2 inch) piece ginger,
*   roughly chopped*
3 cinnamon sticks
4 star anise
1 whole chicken, about 1.5 kg
*   (3 lb 5 oz)*
1/3 cup (80 ml) fish sauce
1/3 cup (80 ml) soy sauce
1 Tbsp soft brown sugar
200 g (7 oz) rice vermicelli noodles
2 cups (230 g) bean sprouts
1 handful mint leaves
1 handful basil leaves
1 lime, quartered
1 fresh red chilli, finely chopped

Preheat the oven to 200°C (400°F). Line a baking tray with baking paper. Put the chopped onion, garlic and ginger on the tray and roast for 30 minutes or until beginning to crisp up. Add the cinnamon and star anise and cook for a further 10 minutes.

Put the chicken in a large stockpot with the roasted onion, garlic, ginger and spices. Add the fish sauce, soy sauce, sugar and enough water to cover the chicken. Bring to the boil over high heat, then reduce the heat to a simmer and cook for 1 hour or until the chicken is cooked through.

Remove the chicken from the stockpot. Strain the stock, discarding the aromatics, then return the stock to the pot. Check and adjust the seasoning – does it need more salt, sweetness or tang?

Once the chicken is cool enough to handle, shred the meat and pop it in a container in the fridge. Return the skin and bones to the stockpot and cook over medium–high heat for a further 1 hour. At this point you can either strain the stock into a container and chill or freeze it, or continue preparing your pho.

Cook the noodles according to the packet instructions, then rinse and divide among four to six bowls. Arrange the bean sprouts and herbs in a serving bowl, and the lime wedges and chilli in another bowl.

Place some of the shredded chicken on top of each pile of noodles and then ladle over the hot chicken stock. Let everyone add their own herbs and other flavourings.

SERVES 4–6

GINGER, LEMON AND TURMERIC SUPER TONIC

I call this a super tonic purely because it tastes super and like a tonic. A shot of this a couple of times a day when you have a cold, are trying to avoid a cold or are on the cusp of one, does seem to help. Make a double batch, keep one for your fridge and give a jar to a sniffly friend.

½ cup (around 80 g) roughly chopped fresh ginger (I scrub it but don't bother with peeling)
¼ cup (around 30 g) fresh turmeric, roughly chopped (see Note)
½ tsp freshly ground black pepper
Juice of 4 lemons
A pinch of cayenne pepper (optional)

Combine all the ingredients in a blender, add ½ cup (125 ml) water and whizz until you have the smoothest paste possible. Add 1 cup (250 ml) water and whizz again. Strain the mixture through a sieve lined with muslin if you like, but I don't mind a bit of texture in this tonic so don't bother. Keep it in the fridge for up to 2 weeks.

To serve, just knock the tonic back as a shot, straight from the fridge, or dilute it with hot water, sweeten with a little honey and sip like a tea.

NOTE
I've seen fresh turmeric popping up at supermarkets, but if it's not at yours, either use 3 teaspoons turmeric paste, or swap it for 2 tablespoons ground turmeric.

MAKES ABOUT 2 CUPS

SPOONFUL OF SUNSHINE ORANGE JELLY

A little pot of cold orange jelly is exactly what I'd like someone to make me next time I'm laid low with the flu or just a miserable cold. Like a little dose of clean sunshine, jelly is a sickbed must – refreshing, tasty, easy to swallow and digest, plus this one is full of vitamin C.

4 cups (1 litre) freshly squeezed orange juice
6 gold-strength gelatine leaves
Juice of 1 lemon (optional – I like the extra tang this gives but if your oranges are tangy enough, leave it out)
1 Tbsp caster sugar, or to taste

Pour 1 cup (250 ml) of the orange juice into a shallow bowl. Add the gelatine leaves and set aside to soak.

Meanwhile, combine the rest of the orange juice with the lemon juice in a small saucepan. Bring to the boil, then remove from the heat and stir in the sugar. Taste for sweetness, adding more sugar if you like. Pour the cold juice and soaked gelatine leaves into the hot juice and whisk until the gelatine has completely dissolved.

Pour the mixture into a jelly mould, bowl or serving glasses, cover and place in the fridge to set, which usually takes about 3–4 hours.

SERVES 4

A pot of cold orange jelly is perfect sick-bed food.

Love bombs

Twice-baked goat's cheese soufflé with apples and almonds ~ Slow-cooked spiced lamb shanks
Chocolate-covered salted caramels ~ Roasted fennel and chilli nuts

Sometimes tragedy just sneaks up on you. A thing happens that makes no sense and makes you feel sick and shocked and bleak. Of course, at times like those, lamb shanks aren't the answer. There is no answer. But people still have to eat, children still need their dinner, and pantries and fridges still need to be stocked.

When grief is at high tide and those everyday needs are forgotten by the affected, it's time for us friends and family to step in. It might be with a tray of lamb shanks ready to heat and serve, or a batch of pre-cooked soufflés that ask for just a dousing in cream and a quick spell in the oven. It might be a grocery shop (and unpack), or you might even let yourself in while they're out and do a quick vacuum, throw a load of washing on and hang out or bring in and fold another. Someone did this for me once and I will never forget it. (Obviously this is only recommended when you actually know the person and are preferably related by blood or years of friendship.)

A lovely lady told me that she and her bestie have a 'love bomb' arrangement for tough times. Whenever the proverbial so-and-so hits the fan, they make dinner, cake, a jar of biscuits or whatever, and leave it at the door, sending a text that says 'incoming love bomb', before driving away. There's no pressure to answer the door, to make conversation and pretend everything is okay, just a recognition that things are hard, and a clear message of support and love with no strings attached. Bombs away.

These will fill your kitchen with
the most comforting smells ever.

TWICE-BAKED GOAT'S CHEESE SOUFFLÉ
WITH APPLES AND ALMONDS

The base of this recipe leans heavily on the one offered in Stephanie Alexander's bible, *The Cook's Companion*. Mum gave me this book when I moved into my first university share house, and I have been cooking from it ever since.

There is so much to love about this dish. Firstly, it is just delicious. Secondly, it can be made completely in advance, even days ahead, then doused in cream and reheated for 15 minutes before serving. And thirdly, the topping of apples and toasted almonds adds texture and brightness that cut effortlessly through the richness. You could cook these as individual soufflés or as one large one, in which case use a 6 cup (1.5 litre) ovenproof dish and increase the cooking time by 5 minutes, if needed.

80 g (2³/4 oz) butter
¹/3 cup (50 g) plain flour
1²/3 cups (420 ml) full-cream milk, warmed
A good pinch of sea salt
3 eggs, separated
1 tsp thyme leaves
³/4 cup (80 g) finely grated parmesan cheese
³/4 cup (90 g) crumbled goat's cheese
2 cups (500 ml) single (pure) cream
2 granny smith apples
¹/2 cup (65 g) slivered almonds

Preheat the oven to 180°C (350°F). Melt the butter in a saucepan over medium–high heat. Dig out six 1 cup (250 ml) moulds or tea cups and brush with a little of the melted butter.

Add the flour to the remaining butter in the saucepan and cook, stirring often, for a few minutes. Pour in the milk, a little at a time, whisking after each addition so you have a thick sauce. Once all the milk is incorporated, cook, stirring often, for 5 more minutes. Remove from the heat, stir in the salt and set aside to cool for a few minutes while you whisk the egg whites until soft peaks form.

Whisk the egg yolks into the milk mixture, then add the thyme, ¹/2 cup (50 g) of the parmesan and all of the goat's cheese. Whisk until smooth, then very, very gently fold in the egg whites.

Divide the mixture among the buttered moulds. Place the moulds in a large roasting tin and pour in boiling water to come three-quarters of the way up the sides of the moulds. Bake for 20 minutes or until the soufflés are puffed and golden. Remove from the water bath and let cool in the moulds for a few minutes before turning out into a greased gratin dish or ovenproof dish. (It doesn't really matter which way up you place the soufflés in the dish.) At this point, you can cover the dish with plastic wrap and pop it in the fridge for up to a day or two. Or you can power on for the second baking.

Pour the cream over the soufflés in the dish, sprinkle with the remaining parmesan and bake for 15 minutes or until golden and puffed up again.

While the soufflés are cooking, slice the apples into matchsticks and toast the almonds.

Top each soufflé with some of the apple and toasted almonds. Serve with a bitter green salad and some bread to mop up the creamy sauce.

SERVES 6

SLOW-COOKED SPICED LAMB SHANKS

Oh, the goodness of these lamb shanks on a cold evening! Correction: oh, the goodness of somebody making you these lamb shanks to reheat and eat on a cold evening, curled up on the couch with a blanket and some nice company (be it a person or a good movie). Make a big batch of these and enjoy them as whole shanks or shred the meat and serve as a ragu with pearl couscous. Or bake the shanks under a blanket of puff pastry, sprinkled with nigella seeds. They're also great done in a slow cooker.

1/3 cup (80 ml) olive oil
8 lamb shanks
2 brown onions, finely diced
4 garlic cloves, finely chopped
4 cm (1 1/2 inch) piece ginger, finely chopped
1 bunch coriander (cilantro), stalks and roots finely chopped, leaves reserved for garnish
1 Tbsp ground cumin
1 Tbsp ground cardamom
1 Tbsp smoked paprika
1 tsp ground cinnamon
1 tsp sea salt
1 cup (250 ml) chicken or vegetable stock
2 x 400 g (14 oz) tins chopped tomatoes
8 dried figs
1/3 cup (80 ml) pomegranate molasses

Preserved lemon yoghurt
4 pieces preserved lemon rind, finely chopped
1/2 cup (130 g) Greek-style yoghurt

Preheat the oven to 150°C (300°F).

Heat some of the olive oil in a large heavy-based saucepan over high heat. Brown the lamb shanks, two or three at a time, for a few minutes on each side or until golden brown, adding more olive oil as necessary. Transfer all of the lamb shanks to a deep roasting tin and set aside.

Reduce the heat, add a little more oil to the pan and cook the onion, stirring often, for 10 minutes or until completely soft. Add the garlic, ginger, coriander stalks and roots, spices and salt to the pan and cook for 5 more minutes. Pour in the stock and tomatoes, then bring to the boil and cook for 5 minutes. Check and adjust the seasoning. Pour the sauce over the lamb shanks, tightly cover the roasting tin with foil and place in the oven for 3 hours or until the meat is lovely and tender. (Alternatively, transfer the lamb shanks and sauce to a slow cooker and cook on low heat for 5 hours. Add the figs and pomegranate molasses and cook for a further 1 hour.)

Remove the roasting tin from the oven and discard the foil. Tuck the dried figs among the lamb shanks and drizzle with the pomegranate molasses. Increase the heat to 180°C (350°F) and return the lamb shanks to the oven for 30 minutes.

Meanwhile, to make the preserved lemon yoghurt, simply mix the two ingredients together and season with a good grinding of black pepper.

At this point, you can either transfer the lamb shanks to a container to freeze or chill, or serve on a bed of sweet potato mash, couscous or rice. Finish with a dollop of the preserved lemon yoghurt and the reserved coriander leaves.

SERVES 8

CHOCOLATE-COVERED SALTED CARAMELS

Home-made chocolate-covered salted caramels – need I say more? Made with love, for your loved ones, they are impressive yet simple to make and always, ALWAYS well received. If you are pressed for time or if confectionery-making of any kind is just not your thing, swing by a nice chocolate shop or deli and buy a good-quality bag of chocolates, caramels or similar. These are lovely and chewy but should be kept cool so they don't go too soft. Don't forget the sprinkle of sea salt – essential.

½ cup (125 ml) single (pure) cream
110 g (3¾ oz) butter
1 cup (220 g) sugar
¼ cup (75 g) liquid glucose (or honey or golden syrup if that's what you have at hand)
450 g (1 lb) milk chocolate
Sea salt flakes, for sprinkling

Before you start, measure out all the ingredients and lightly oil and line a 21 x 13 cm (8¼ x 5 inch) loaf tin.

Combine the cream and butter in a small saucepan over medium–high heat. Cook, stirring often, until the butter has melted and the mixture reaches boiling point (don't let it boil and bubble over the pan – that's messy and annoying for you). Set aside.

Now combine ¼ cup (60 ml) water with the sugar and liquid glucose in another saucepan over medium–high heat. Try not to let the sugar splash up the side of the pan or it may crystallise later on and make the caramels grainy. Heat to boiling point and, using a pastry brush dipped in water, give the side of the saucepan a little brush to ensure no sugar crystals are lurking. Pop a sugar thermometer into the pan and cook until the mixture reaches 173°C (343°F) – it will turn a lovely amber colour. At this point, pour in the hot cream mixture in a slow, steady stream and use the thermometer to stir the mixture together. Be careful as it will all bubble up like crazy. Return the thermometer to the side of the saucepan and cook again until the mixture reaches 118°C (244°F).

Pour the caramel into the loaf tin and place in the fridge to firm up for at least 2 hours. It should be firm enough to cut at this point. Turn out onto a board and cut into even squares or bars. Place these on a tray lined with baking paper so they are sitting a little apart.

Melt the chocolate in a bowl over a saucepan of simmering water. Using two forks, dip a piece of caramel into the chocolate and swirl it around so it is completely covered, then return to the tray and sprinkle with sea salt. (You could just get a fork and dip it into the melted chocolate, then drizzle it over the caramels – this is a much easier approach and while it doesn't give a completely covered caramel, it also looks and tastes great.) Repeat with the remaining caramels. Store in the fridge.

MAKES ABOUT 20

ROASTED FENNEL AND CHILLI NUTS

These are a total winner, very more-ish and great to send someone for a little thank you or similar. They are also fabulous bashed up a bit and sprinkled over salads, such as Pearl barley, beetroot and yoghurt salad (page 29). You could even post them, but do so in a plastic container or bag inside a box. Glass jars are pretty but breakable!

Vegetable oil, for greasing
¼ cup (55 g) caster sugar
1 Tbsp sea salt
1 tsp ground chilli or chilli flakes
1 Tbsp fennel seeds
2 egg whites
4 cups (about 560 g) nuts (I went
* with almonds and walnuts, but*
* you could substitute cashews,*
* macadamias, pecans, etc.)*

Preheat the oven to 150°C (300°F). Rub a large baking tray with a little vegetable oil.

Put the sugar, salt, chilli and fennel seeds in a small bowl and mix well.

In a separate, larger bowl, whisk the egg whites until frothy. Add the nuts and the sugar mixture to the egg whites and gently fold to combine.

Spread the nut mixture over the tray and pop in the oven for 40 minutes, mixing everything around halfway through. Turn off the oven but leave the tray in there to cool (scrape the mixture off the bottom of the tray after about 10 minutes to make sure it doesn't stick while cooling). Store the nuts in a jar or airtight container.

MAKES ABOUT 4 CUPS

When life gives you lemons

Sour citrus rinds ~ Ruby grapefruit, orange and barley cordial
Lemon and passionfruit curd ~ Citrus simmer pots

Eating seasonally makes extra sense in the middle of winter when citrus fruits are
at their best and bursting with bright, tangy juice and cold-busting vitamin C. If you're
lucky enough to have a lemon, orange or lime tree (or have access to one), stock up
and get squeezing. Freeze the juice in ice-cube trays so you can have
juicy times and make these recipes all year round.

SOUR CITRUS RINDS

These are a home-made, far superior version of those horrible but weirdly addictive sour worm sweets you buy in packets from the petrol station on road trips. They aren't for everyone, though – my daughter and I LOVE them but my husband and son think they're horrible. If you like really sour sweets and flavours, these are for you.

4 oranges, 2 limes, 2 lemons and 2 pink grapefruit (or any other combination of citrus fruits you fancy, so you have about 10 pieces in total)
2¹/₂ cups (550 g) caster sugar
2 Tbsp citric acid

Halve the citrus fruits and gently scrape out the flesh. (Reserve the flesh for juice or the curd on page 58.) Cut the rind halves into 1 cm (¹/₂ inch) thick strips.

Fill a saucepan with water and bring to the boil. Add the rinds and boil for 10 minutes. Drain, then fill the saucepan with fresh water and bring to the boil again. Return the rinds to the pan to boil for 10 minutes.

Drain the rinds and return them to the empty pan with 2 cups (440 g) of the sugar and 3 cups (750 ml) water. Bring to the boil and cook for 30 minutes, then drain. Arrange the rinds on a rack set over a baking tray lined with baking paper. Place in the fridge until completely cool.

Combine the citric acid and remaining sugar in a large bowl. Toss the rinds in the sugar, then return to the drying rack, reserving the sugar, and leave at room temperature for 30 minutes (make sure you keep them away from ants). Toss the rinds in the sugar one more time, then return to the rack to dry out overnight, or for at least 8 hours. Once completely dry, store the rinds in an airtight container.

NOTE
Don't be tempted to put these in a low oven to dry out like I did: sticky city.

MAKES ABOUT 2 CUPS

RUBY GRAPEFRUIT, ORANGE AND BARLEY CORDIAL

This is just gorgeous with mineral water, ice and a slice of lemon or orange. Or mix it with boiling water and serve as a lovely warm drink.

1¹/₄ cups (250 g) pearl barley
1¹/₄ cups (310 ml) freshly squeezed ruby grapefruit juice
1¹/₄ cups (310 ml) freshly squeezed orange juice
3 cups (660 g) sugar
³/₄ cup (250 g) honey
1 vanilla bean, split lengthways

Toast the barley in a large saucepan over medium–high heat, stirring often so the grains don't burn, for 5 minutes or until it turns a lovely golden colour.

Stir in the remaining ingredients and 4 cups (1 litre) water. Bring to the boil, then reduce the heat and simmer for 10 minutes. Leave to cool for 5 minutes, then strain the cordial into jars. Store in the fridge for up to 2 weeks.

MAKES ABOUT 3 CUPS

LEMON AND PASSIONFRUIT CURD

This is a lovely curd recipe: it uses whole eggs, which is nice and neat, sets well and tastes gorgeous. What it does ask for is a little time, so please keep the heat low, stir almost constantly and watch carefully. The quantities given here make quite a lot of curd but I think if you are going to spend 20 minutes stirring, you may as well get a good few jars for your trouble. If you prefer to make just lemon curd, leave out the passionfruit and add one more lemon.

220 g (7³/4 oz) unsalted butter
1²/3 cups (370 g) caster sugar
Grated zest and juice of 4 lemons –
    you need ³/4 cup (185 ml) juice
6 eggs, lightly beaten
¹/2 cup (125 g) passionfruit pulp
    (you'll need about 4 passionfruit)

Put the butter, sugar and lemon zest in a glass bowl resting over a saucepan of simmering water. Cook, stirring often, for about 5 minutes until the butter has melted and the sugar has dissolved.

Add the eggs, lemon juice and passionfruit pulp and cook, gently whisking, for 20 minutes or until the mixture has thickened and coats the back of a wooden spoon – if you have a sugar thermometer, setting point will be around 80°C (176°F). Spoon into clean jars, seal and keep in the fridge for up to 2 weeks.

MAKES ABOUT 5 CUPS

THINGS TO DO WITH CURD

~ Fill store-bought or home-made sweet pastry tart shells with curd and top with a dollop of thick or whipped cream.
~ Make the Fluffy pancakes from page 34 and serve with Poached quinces (page 75) and a dollop of curd.
~ Serve the curd with meringues and whipped cream.

OTHER CURD FLAVOURS

~ Orange curd

~ Blood-orange curd

~ Lime curd

~ Raspberry curd – blitz 1 cup (125 g) raspberries, push through a sieve and then fold through the cooled curd

CITRUS SIMMER POTS

A bright, clean aroma in the kitchen can make a world of difference to your mood, so, instead of forking out for a scented candle, air freshener or burning incense, consider one of these simmer pots. They cost next to nothing, are completely natural and put much-needed moisture back into the air (especially welcome when you have the fire or heater going constantly).

Simply place the ingredients for your chosen simmer pot in a small saucepan, cover with water (it should come about three-quarters of the way up the side of the pan) and simmer, topping up the water as needed, for a few hours.

To make these up as a gift, combine all the ingredients in a jar or cellophane bag and pop in a little instruction card.

LEMON, ROSEMARY AND VANILLA

1 lemon, thinly sliced
2 rosemary sprigs
1 vanilla bean, split lengthways (scrape the seeds into the water and add the vanilla bean as well)

GRAPEFRUIT AND EUCALYPTUS

Peel of 1 grapefruit, cut into wide strips
5–6 eucalyptus leaves (crush the leaves before adding them to the pan to release their oils)

MANDARIN AND LAVENDER

Peel of 1 mandarin, cut into wide strips
3 fresh or dried lavender flower heads

SPICED ORANGE

Peel of 1 orange, cut into wide strips
2 bay leaves
2 cinnamon sticks
2 cloves
1 nutmeg

The aroma of these simmer pots will brighten both your room and your mood.

Sweet winter afternoons

Basic sweet dough ~ Sweet Christmas wreath with blood-orange curd
Hot chocolate ~ Milk buns ~ Cinnamon scrolls ~ Cultured butter

For me, baking with soft, buttery yeasted doughs is the sweetest of meditations.
The basic dough on the page opposite feels so good to knead, plait and shape, and it
yields the most delicious, comforting buns, scrolls and wreaths. And then there's the
ritual of resting the dough, gently shaping it, resting again, brushing with egg wash,
sprinkling with sugar or dusting with cinnamon. If you haven't done much baking
with yeast, please start here and hopefully you'll see what I mean!

BASIC SWEET DOUGH

This is one of my favourite recipes. The dough is silky smooth and lovely to work with, and it can be made into many delightful forms, including a large twisted Christmas wreath filled with blood-orange curd (see over). The sweet little Milk buns with Hot chocolate are hard to resist, as are the classic Cinnamon scrolls (pages 68–69).

1 cup (250 ml) milk
100 g (3¹/₂ oz) butter
3 tsp dried yeast
¹/₄ cup (55 g) caster sugar
1 egg
3¹/₃ cups (500 g) plain flour,
  plus extra for dusting
A pinch of salt

Combine the milk and butter in a small saucepan. Heat, stirring, until the milk is warm and the butter has melted. Remove from the heat and set aside to cool until lukewarm.

Tip the milk and butter mixture into the bowl of an electric mixer with a dough attachment.

Add the yeast, sugar, egg, flour and salt and knead for 5 minutes. Turn out onto a lightly floured work surface and finish kneading by hand for a minute or so. (You can do the entire kneading process by hand if you prefer – combine the dry ingredients on a work surface, make a well in the centre and then add the milk and butter mixture and the egg, and knead together.)

Place the dough in a lightly oiled bowl, cover with a tea towel and leave in a warm place for 1 hour or until doubled in size.

MAKES ENOUGH FOR ONE LARGE TWISTED WREATH, 10 MILK BUNS OR 12 CINNAMON SCROLLS

SWEET CHRISTMAS WREATH WITH BLOOD-ORANGE CURD

This wreath is a really lovely recipe to bake and share on a cold winter's afternoon. For the curd, follow the recipe for Lemon and passionfruit curd on page 58, but swap two of the lemons with blood oranges.

Serve the wreath warm with Rhubarb compote (page 75) and a little thick cream or just a little extra blood-orange curd.

1 quantity basic sweet dough
  (page 65)
Grated zest of 2 oranges
1 cup (250 ml) blood-orange curd
1 Tbsp single (pure) cream
1 egg
Icing sugar, for dusting

Make the dough according to the recipe, adding the orange zest with the flour and other dry ingredients before kneading.

Once the dough has risen, gently turn it out onto a lightly floured work surface. Roll the dough into a large rectangle, then transfer to a baking tray lined with baking paper, cover with plastic wrap and place in the fridge for 1 hour. This will make the twisting part much easier.

Preheat the oven to 200°C (400°F).

Spread the dough with the blood-orange curd. Roll the dough from the longest edge into a long sausage, then cut it in half lengthways to make two long half-cylinders. Place the halves next to each other, cut sides up, and twist together into a braid, pressing the ends together. This can take a bit of practice but it's fun and isn't tricky once you get the idea.

Whisk the cream and egg together to make an egg wash. Gently transfer the wreath to the lined baking tray and brush with the egg wash. Bake for 10 minutes, then reduce the heat to 180°C (350°F) and bake for a further 25 minutes or until the wreath is golden brown. Serve warm, dusted with icing sugar.

SERVES 8

This is delicious warm from the oven with a little extra blood-orange curd.

HOT CHOCOLATE

Pour 1 cup (250 ml) milk per person into a saucepan. Warm over medium heat until just boiling. Remove the pan from the heat and stir in ¼ cup (35 g) roughly chopped chocolate per person (I use milk chocolate for the kids and a nice dark chocolate for me).

MILK BUNS

My maternal grandfather was Danish and my fondest memory of visiting Copenhagen was arriving at our hotel on a cold-to-the-bone afternoon to find a tray of warm milk buns set up in a cosy, fire-lit corner of the lobby. With the buns was a jug of hot chocolate, a bowl of cream and a smaller bowl of chocolate coffee beans. Heaven.

I can't think of a more comforting thing to make and deliver to a friend or family who are having a difficult time. Children in particular adore this combination. Serve the buns warm (or reheated) within a day or two of baking.

1 quantity basic sweet dough (page 65)
2 tsp ground cardamom
1 egg
2 Tbsp single (pure) cream
1/3 cup (75 g) caster sugar

Make the dough according to the recipe, adding the cardamom with the flour and other dry ingredients before kneading.

Once the dough has risen, turn it out onto a lightly floured work surface and give it a light knead. Cut the dough into 10 equal pieces and shape into neat balls. Place on a baking tray lined with baking paper and leave to rise again for 30 minutes.

Preheat the oven to 200°C (400°F). Whisk the egg and cream together and gently brush over the buns. Sprinkle with the sugar and bake for 15–20 minutes or until risen and golden. Serve the buns warm with hot chocolate.

MAKES 10

CINNAMON SCROLLS

The smell of these baking in the oven is balm for the senses – cinnamon scrolls are like a bear hug, in food form. And like any yeasted baking project, the satisfaction value when pulling these golden beauties out of the oven is off the charts.

1 quantity basic sweet dough (page 65)
100 g (3 1/2 oz) butter, softened
1/2 cup (110 g) firmly packed soft brown sugar
1 Tbsp ground cinnamon
1 egg
1 Tbsp single (pure) cream

Roll the dough out on a lightly floured work surface into a rectangle, about 35 x 25 cm (14 x 10 inches).

Put the butter, brown sugar and cinnamon in a bowl and mix until well combined. Spread the butter over the dough (I usually start with the back of a spoon and then use my fingers to spread it to cover the whole rectangle).

Gently roll the dough from the longest edge of the rectangle into a long sausage. Cut the sausage into 4 cm (1 1/2 inch) pieces and place on a lined baking tray, swirly side up, leaving 1 cm (1/2 inch) between each one so they can spread as they cook. Leave to rise for about 30 minutes.

Preheat the oven to 200°C (400°F). Whisk the egg and cream together to make an egg wash. Brush the rolls with the egg wash, then cook in the oven for 20 minutes or until golden.

MAKES ABOUT 12

CULTURED BUTTER

So easy, so delicious and so impressive, home-made cultured butter is completely different to what you buy in the shops. Plus, you end up not only with fresh, delicious butter but also a bottle of home-made buttermilk to bake with.

Check the label of the cream to ensure it contains no thickeners or preservatives – a good non-homogenised cream is ideal, otherwise a carton of thin, pure cream will be fine.

4 cups (1 litre) single (pure) cream
1/2 cup (130 g) Greek-style yoghurt with live cultures
1/2 tsp sea salt

You'll need a stand mixer with a whisk attachment. Combine the cream and yoghurt in the bowl, cover with plastic wrap and leave in the fridge overnight.

Place the bowl on the stand mixer and cover the top of the bowl with plastic wrap so nothing can splash out while mixing. Don't skip this step – you'll regret it when you're cleaning curd and buttermilk off the ceiling! Begin whisking, and keep going until you see the mixture separate into clumps of butter and buttermilk. Pour the buttermilk into a sterilised bottle and store it in the fridge for up to 3 days.

Bring all of the butter together in your hands and mix in the salt, then rinse under cold running water to wash away as much buttermilk as possible.

Now, you want to 'work the curds' on a clean wooden surface. This simply means rolling and working the butter between your hands to remove the moisture. Form the butter into a log shape, wrap it in baking paper and keep in the fridge for up to a week.

MAKES ABOUT 350 G (12 OZ) BUTTER

Compound butter

To really gild the lily, you could take your beautiful cultured butter and turn it into a compound butter, which is essentially flavoured butter. Below are four ideas you could try, but the options really are endless. One more idea: divide the cultured butter into four portions and flavour each as suggested below, then wrap up, label and give away with a few serving ideas. I'd love to receive that little gift; it could lead to so many good, easy meals that I might not even think of if preoccupied with life's more messy moments.

~ Truffle butter
Grate a small black truffle into the soft butter with a little sea salt, then form into a gloriously scented log.

~ Cinnamon and maple syrup butter
Mix 1 tablespoon maple syrup and 1/2 teaspoon ground cinnamon into 100 g (3 1/2 oz) soft butter. Serve spread on pancakes and waffles. Or peel and halve a few apples or pears, cut out the cores and fill with 1 tablespoon of the butter. Arrange in a roasting tin, splash a little white wine or water into the dish and roast until the fruit is completely soft.

~ Sage and orange butter
Mix 2 tablespoons finely chopped sage, the grated zest of 1 orange and a good grinding of black pepper into 100 g (3 1/2 oz) soft butter. Spread on warm dinner rolls; spoon into baked potatoes; toss with steamed green beans; or dollop on top of grilled chicken breasts.

~ Anchovy and caper butter
Mix 3 finely chopped anchovies, 3 finely chopped capers and 3 finely chopped garlic cloves into 100 g (3 1/2 oz) soft butter. Add half a handful each of finely chopped flat-leaf parsley and chives. Serve on top of an indulgent, barbecued rib-eye or scotch fillet steak or baked salmon fillet.

SPICY, SMOKY BEEF RAGU

$^1/_3$ cup (80 ml) olive oil
2 onions, finely chopped
4 garlic cloves, finely chopped
1 tsp thyme leaves
2 chorizo sausages, very finely chopped (I give them
  a whizz in the food processor)
800 g (1 lb 12 oz) chuck steak or other
  slow-cooking cut, cut into small pieces (your
  butcher should be happy to do this, otherwise
  use beef mince)
1 cup (250 ml) full-bodied red wine
2 x 400 g (14 oz) tins whole tomatoes
$^1/_3$ cup (90 g) tomato paste (concentrated purée)
4 chipotle chillies in adobo sauce, roughly
  chopped (you can usually find these in the
  Mexican section of the supermarket)
1 Tbsp soft brown sugar
1 Tbsp balsamic vinegar
1 tsp salt

Preheat the oven to 140°C (275°F). Heat the oil in a
large heavy-based ovenproof saucepan or flameproof
casserole dish over medium heat. Add the onion, garlic
and thyme and cook, stirring occasionally, for about
10 minutes or until softened.

Add the chorizo, increase the heat to high and cook
for a few minutes. Next add the beef and cook for a
few more minutes. Pour in the wine and let it bubble
down and reduce a little. Add the tomatoes, tomato
paste, chillies, sugar, vinegar and salt and stir well.

Transfer to the oven for 4 hours, by which time it
will be a rich, deeply flavoured pot of goodness. Stir
the ragu every now and then during cooking so that
it doesn't stick to the bottom of the pan.

SERVES 6–8

GROUND TOASTED CARDAMOM

$^1/_3$ cup (35 g) cardamom pods

Preheat the oven to 140°C (275°F). Scatter the
cardamom pods over a baking tray and bake for
10 minutes or until beginning to turn dark green.
Cool, then transfer to a high-powered blender,
food processor, spice grinder or coffee grinder
and blitz as finely as possible. Pass through a
sieve to remove any larger pieces.

Store in an airtight container as the best ground
cardamom ever.

MAKES ABOUT 1$^1/_2$ TABLESPOONS

SWEET DUKKAH

$^1/_2$ cup (75 g) hazelnuts or walnuts
$^1/_3$ cup (50 g) sesame seeds
2 Tbsp poppy seeds
$^1/_2$ tsp coriander seeds
$^2/_3$ cup (100 g) raw unsalted pistachio nuts
$^1/_2$ tsp ground toasted cardamom (see above)
$^1/_2$ tsp ground cinnamon
$^1/_4$ tsp ground nutmeg
2 Tbsp soft brown sugar
A pinch of sea salt

Preheat the oven to 180°C (350°F). Spread the
hazelnuts or walnuts on a baking tray and toast for
5 minutes. Add the sesame seeds, poppy seeds and
coriander seeds and continue to toast for another
5 minutes. Remove from the oven.

Combine the hazelnuts or walnuts and pistachios in a
food processor or use a mortar and pestle and blitz or
bash until the mixture resembles coarse breadcrumbs.
Add the toasted seeds, spices, brown sugar and salt.
Give it another quick blitz or bash and mix to combine,
then store in a jar or airtight container.

MAKES ABOUT 1$^1/_2$ CUPS

SALTED CARAMEL SAUCE

1¾ cups (390 g) caster sugar
170 g (5¾ oz) unsalted butter, cut into cubes
1 cup (250 ml) single (pure) cream
Seeds from 1 vanilla bean
1 tsp sea salt

Put the sugar in a saucepan over medium–high heat
and cook, stirring often, until it melts into a smooth
caramel (watch it carefully towards the end because
it can go from perfectly golden to burnt in the blink
of an eye). As soon as the sugar is completely melted
and smooth, add the butter and whisk until it has
melted into a smooth sauce.

Remove the pan from the heat. Whisk in the cream,
vanilla seeds and salt. Return to the heat and bring
to the boil. Cook, stirring often, for 5 minutes, then
remove from the heat and divide among jars. Store
in the fridge for up to a month.

NOTE
The sauce thickens up quite a lot in the fridge. To
soften it, either place the jar in a bowl of hot water,
give it a quick zap in the microwave or transfer it
to a saucepan and gently warm it until it loosens up.

MAKES ABOUT 2 CUPS

RHUBARB COMPOTE

1 bunch (300 g/10½ oz) rhubarb, trimmed
1 vanilla bean, split lengthways
Juice of 2 oranges
⅓ cup (75 g) caster sugar

Preheat the oven to 180°C (350°F). Line a small
roasting tin with baking paper. Cut the rhubarb into
3 cm (1¼ inch) batons and add to the tin with the
vanilla bean, orange juice and sugar. Toss well, then
cover with foil and roast for 25 minutes or until the
rhubarb has completely collapsed.

MAKES ABOUT 2 CUPS

POACHED QUINCES

2 cups (440 g) sugar
Juice of 1 lemon
1 Tbsp vanilla bean paste
1 cinnamon stick
4–6 quinces, peel, cored and quartered,
    cores reserved

Preheat the oven to 150°C (300°F).

Combine the sugar, lemon juice, vanilla bean paste
and cinnamon in a saucepan and bring to the boil.
Stir over medium heat until the sugar has dissolved,
then simmer for a few minutes.

Meanwhile, arrange the quince pieces in a deep
roasting tin in a single layer. Don't worry if they
colour a little – this won't affect the end result.
Tie the cores together in a piece of muslin and
add it to the tin (I never seem to have any muslin
on hand, so I just scatter a few cores over the top
of the quinces then fish them out later). The cores
will add colour and pectin to the fruit.

Pour the sugar syrup over the quinces and cover
tightly with foil. Place in the oven for 3–4 hours or
until the quinces have turned a ruby-red colour and
are deliciously aromatic. Remove and discard the
cores and cinnamon stick.

MAKES ABOUT 2 CUPS

ACKNOWLEDGEMENTS

This book is for Tim, Alice and Tom. Our little family is everything to me. Thank you, guys, for your love and support, and, right back at you.

As anyone whose primary income depends on primary industry knows, the farming life can be really hard. It's a juggle, a gamble and a 24 hour/ 7 days a week job. And yes, it's a cliche, but despite the challenges we do look around us every day and feel grateful we get to live here on this farm, in this place together. Thank you, Tim and ALL of the farmers who grow and produce our food, for keeping the boat afloat through drought, bushfires, all the uncertainties and challenges.

Thank you to my parents, Annie and Henry Herron, whose beautiful property features prominently throughout this book. Thank you for giving my siblings and me confidence, opportunity and a home we always love to come back to.

Thank you to the team at Murdoch Books, especially Corinne Roberts who has guided me through this process with such skill and warmth, and designer Vivien Valk who has worked so hard to make this book so beautiful.

Big thanks to Josie Chapman for opening up her beautiful cottages at the Old Convent B&B Borenore for some of the photography.

Making and sharing good, simple, seasonal food is an act of love and generosity, so my final thanks is to you, for buying this book and hopefully taking inspiration from it to go out and leave a basket of home-made food at someone's door soon. It will mean so much to them.

This edition published in 2020 by Murdoch Books, an imprint of Allen & Unwin
Content originally published in *A Basket by the Door*, published in 2019 by Murdoch Books

Murdoch Books UK
Ormond House, 26–27 Boswell Street,
London, WC1N 3JZ
Phone: +44 (0) 20 8785 5995
murdochbooks.co.uk
info@murdochbooks.co.uk

For corporate orders & custom publishing contact our business development team at salesenquiries@murdochbooks.com.au

Publisher: Corinne Roberts
Cover design: northwoodgreen.com
Internal design: Vivien Valk
Editor: Justine Harding
Production director: Lou Playfair

Photography: Sophie Hansen, except page 2 by Lina Hayes

ISBN 978 1 911 63282 5

A catalogue record for this book is available from the British Library

Printed by C&C Offset Printing Co Ltd, China

TABLESPOONS: We have used Australian 20 ml (4 teaspoon) tablespoon measures. If you are using a smaller European 15 ml (3 teaspoon) tablespoon, add an extra teaspoon of the ingredient for each tablespoon specified in the recipe.

10 9 8 7 6 5 4 3 2 1

MIX
Paper from responsible sources
FSC® C008047

The paper in this book is FSC® certified. FSC® promotes environmentally responsible, socially beneficial and economically viable management of the world's forests.

This edition published in 2020 by Murdoch Books, an imprint of Allen & Unwin
Content originally published in *A Basket by the Door*, published in 2019 by Murdoch Books

Murdoch Books UK
Ormond House, 26–27 Boswell Street,
London, WC1N 3JZ
Phone: +44 (0) 20 8785 5995
murdochbooks.co.uk
info@murdochbooks.co.uk

For corporate orders & custom publishing contact our business development team at salesenquiries@murdochbooks.com.au

Publisher: Corinne Roberts
Cover design: northwoodgreen.com
Internal design: Vivien Valk
Editor: Justine Harding
Production director: Lou Playfair

Photography: Sophie Hansen, except page 2 by Lina Hayes

ISBN 978 1 911 63282 5

A catalogue record for this book is available from the British Library

Printed by C&C Offset Printing Co Ltd, China

TABLESPOONS: We have used Australian 20 ml (4 teaspoon) tablespoon measures. If you are using a smaller European 15 ml (3 teaspoon) tablespoon, add an extra teaspoon of the ingredient for each tablespoon specified in the recipe.

10 9 8 7 6 5 4 3 2 1